MW00941444

# Oreo Creations

Creative Uses for Everyone's Favorite Cookie

## By

## Angel Burns

# License Notices

# Get Your Daily Deals Here!

**Free books on me!** Subscribe now to receive free and discounted books directly to your email. This means you will always have choices of your next book from the comfort of your own home and a reminder email will pop up a few days beforehand, so you never miss out! Every day, free books will make their way into your inbox and all you need to do is choose what you want.

What could be better than that?

Fill out the box below to get started on this amazing offer and start receiving your daily deals right away!

## https://angel-burns.gr8.com

# Table of Contents

# Easy and Delicious Oreo Recipes

HHHHHHHHHHHHHHHHHHHHHHHHHHHHHHHHHHHHHH

# Recipe 1: Golden Oreo Fudge

If you love the taste of golden Oreos, then this is an Oreo dish I know you will want to make. Easy to make and even easier to eat, this is a dish you will want to make every day.

**Yield:** 64 servings

**Preparation Time:** 3 hours and 20 minutes

## Ingredient List:

- 1 ½ cups of white sugar
- 6 Tablespoons of butter
- 1/3 cup of evaporated milk
- 1 cup of marshmallow crème
- 1 ¼ cups of white chocolate chips
- ½ teaspoons of pure vanilla
- 10 to 12 Golden Oreos, crumbled
- ¼ cup of rainbow sprinkles

HHHHHHHHHHHHHHHHHHHHHHHHHHHHHHHHHHH

**Instructions:**

1. Place a sheet of aluminum foil into a baking dish.

2. In a saucepan set over medium heat, add in the white sugar, butter and evaporated milk. Whisk well to mix. Cook for 3 minutes. Allow to come to a boil. Boil for 1 minutes. Remove from heat.

3. Add in the marshmallow crème and white chocolate chips. Stir well until smooth in consistency.

4. Add in the pure vanilla. Stir well until incorporated.

5. Crumble 5 to 6 Oreos and add into the mix. Fold gently to incorporate.

6. Spread into the baking dish. Top off with the remaining crumbled Oreos and rainbow sprinkles.

7. Cover and place into the fridge to chill for 3 to 4 hours.

8. Slice into squares and serve.

# Recipe 2: Oreo Cheesecakeadilla

This is a crafty and unique way to use Oreo cookies in your next dessert dish. This is one Oreo dish I know you will quickly become addicted to.

**Yield:** 1 serving

**Preparation Time:** 10 minutes

## Ingredient List:

- 1/3 cup of soft cream cheese
- ¼ cup of Oreo cookies, crushed and extra for garnish
- 2, 8 inch flour tortillas
- Butter, for greasing
- 1 teaspoon of white sugar

HHHHHHHHHHHHHHHHHHHHHHHHHHHHHHHHHHHH

## Instructions:

1. Place a skillet over medium heat.

2. In a bowl, add in the soft cream cheese and crushed Oreos. Stir well to mix.

3. Grease the outside of the flour tortillas with the butter. On one tortilla side, add the Oreo mix. Place into the skillet with the Oreo mix facing up. Top off with the second flour tortilla.

4. Cook for 3 minutes or until crispy. Gently flip and continue to cook for an additional 2 minutes.

5. Transfer onto a plate. Sprinkle the white sugar over the top.

6. Top off with extra crushed Oreos and serve immediately.

# Recipe 3: Cookies and Cream Doughnuts

The very sight of these doughnuts will be sure to send your family into a feeding frenzy. They are so mouthwatering, the very smell of them will send your family running to the kitchen.

**Yield:** 12 servings

**Preparation Time:** 1 hour

**Ingredients for the doughnuts:**

- 2/3 cup of powdered cocoa
- 1 ¾ cups of white flour
- 1 cup of light brown sugar
- 1 teaspoon of baker's style baking powder
- 1 teaspoon of baker's style baking soda
- ¾ teaspoons of salt
- 2 eggs
- ¾ cup of whole milk
- 2 teaspoons of pure vanilla
- 2 teaspoons of white vinegar
- 1 stick of butter, melted

**Ingredients for the icing:**

- 2 cups of powdered sugar
- 4 Tablespoons of whole milk
- 1 teaspoon of pure vanilla
- 8 Oreo cookies, crushed

HHHHHHHHHHHHHHHHHHHHHHHHHHHHHHHHHHHH

**Instructions:**

1. Preheat the oven to 350 degrees. Grease a doughnut pan with cooking spray.

2. Prepare the doughnuts. In a bowl, add in the powdered cocoa, white flour, white sugar, salt, baking powder and soda. Stir well to mix.

3. In a separate bowl, add in the eggs, whole milk, pure vanilla and white vinegar. Whisk well until lightly beaten. Pour into the flour mix and stir well until just mixed.

4. Pour the batter into the doughnut pan.

5. Place into the oven to bake for 10 to 15 minutes or until baked through. Remove and set aside to cool.

6. Prepare the icing. In a bowl, add in the powdered sugar, whole milk and pure vanilla. Whisk well until smooth in consistency.

7. Dip the top portion of the doughnuts into the icing. Place onto a wire rack.

8. Sprinkle the crushed Oreos immediately over the top.

9. Set aside to rest for 20 minutes or until the glaze is set.

10. Serve.

# Recipe 4: Oreo Pancakes

There is no other pancake recipe that is quite as delicious as this dish. Not only can it help satisfy your sweet tooth, but it is a perfect way to start your morning as well.

**Yield:** 4 servings

**Preparation Time:** 20 minutes

**Ingredient List:**

- 1 ½ cup of white flour
- ¼ cup of powdered unsweetened dark cocoa
- ½ cup of white sugar
- 2 teaspoons of baker's style baking powder
- 1 ¼ cup of whole milk
- 1 egg
- 2 Tablespoons of butter, melted and extra for greasing
- Dash of salt
- Whipped cream, for serving
- Oreos, crushed and for serving
- Chocolate sauce, for drizzling

HHHHHHHHHHHHHHHHHHHHHHHHHHHHHHHHHHHH

**Instructions:**

1. In a bowl, add in the white flour, powdered cocoa, white sugar and baker's style baking powder. Whisk well to mix.

2. In a separate bowl, add in the whole milk, egg and melted butter. Whisk well until evenly mixed. Pour into the flour mix. Stir well until just mixed.

3. In a skillet set over medium heat, add in 1 tablespoon of butter. Add ¼ cup of the pancake batter into the skillet. Cook for 5 minutes or until cooked through. Transfer onto a plate and repeat.

4. Serve the pancakes with a dollop of whipped cream, the crushed Oreos and a drizzle of the chocolate sauce.

# Recipe 5: Cookies and Cream Cookies

If you love the taste of cookies and cream chocolate bars, then this is a cookie dish that you will fall in love with. Made with Oreo cookies and cookies and cream pudding, this is a dish that will please everyone who tries a bite of it.

**Yield:** 36 servings

**Preparation Time:** 35 minutes

**Ingredient List:**

- ¾ cup of butter, soft
- ½ cup of light brown sugar
- ½ cup of white sugar
- 2 eggs
- 1 teaspoon of pure vanilla
- 1, 4.2 ounce pack of cookies and cream pudding mix
- 1 teaspoon of baker's style baking soda
- 2 ¼ cup of white flour
- ¼ teaspoons of salt
- 8 Oreo cookies, crushed
- 5 ounces of Cookies and crème chocolate bar, chopped

HHHHHHHHHHHHHHHHHHHHHHHHHHHHHHHHHHH

**Instructions:**

1. Preheat the oven to 350 degrees.

2. In a bowl, add in the soft butter, white sugar and light brown sugar. Beat with an electric mixer until fluffy in consistency. Add in the eggs and pure vanilla. Continue to beat until smooth in consistency.

3. In a separate bowl, add in the cookies and cream pudding mix, white flour, dash of salt and baker's style baking soda. Stir well to mix. Add into the butter mix. Stir to mix. Add in the chocolate bar and fold gently to incorporate.

4. Shape the mix into balls that are 1 to 2 inches in size. Place onto a baking sheet.

5. Place into the oven to bake for 10 to 12 minutes or until the cookies are set. Remove and cool for 10 minutes before serving.

# Recipe 6: Oreo Chip Cookies

If you love the taste of classic chocolate chip cookies, then this is one Oreo dish that you are going to want to make as often as possible.

**Yield:** 15 servings

**Preparation Time:** 30 minutes

**Ingredient List:**

- 2 sticks of butter, soft
- 1 cup of white sugar
- 1 cup of light brown sugar
- 2 eggs
- 2 teaspoons of pure vanilla
- 1 teaspoon of baker's style baking soda
- 2 ½ cups of white flour
- 1 teaspoon of salt
- 1 ½ cup of chocolate wafer cookies, crushed

HHHHHHHHHHHHHHHHHHHHHHHHHHHHHHHHHH

**Instructions:**

1. Preheat the oven to 350 degrees. Place a sheet of parchment paper onto two baking sheets.

2. In a bowl, add in the soft butter, white sugar and light brown sugar. Beat with an electric mixer until fluffy in consistency. Add in the eggs and pure vanilla. Continue to beat until smooth in consistency.

3. In a bowl, add in the baker's style baking soda, white flour and dash of salt. Stir well until mixed. Add into the butter mix. Stir well until just mixed.

4. Drop the cookie dough by the tablespoon onto the baking sheets.

5. Place into the oven to bake for 10 to 12 minutes or until golden.

6. Remove and set aside on a wire rack to cool completely before serving.

# Recipe 7: Oreo Brownie Ice Cream Cake

While this is a cake that will take some time to prepare, the end result is well worth it. It is perfect to make whenever you need a special treat to serve during your next holiday event.

**Yield:** 8 servings

**Preparation Time:** 6 hours and 30 minutes

**Ingredients for the brownie layer:**

- 1, box of brownie mix
- 2 eggs
- ¼ cup of water
- ½ cup of vegetable oil

**Ingredients for the cookie dough layer:**

- 1 sticks of butter, melted
- 1/3 cup of light brown sugar
- ¼ cup of white sugar
- 2 Tablespoons of whole milk
- ½ teaspoons of pure vanilla
- 1 ¼ cup of white flour
- ¼ teaspoons of salt
- 1 cup of miniature chocolate chips

**Ingredients for the Oreo:**

- 1 sleeve of Oreo cookies

**Ingredients for the ice cream:**

- 1 gallon of cookies and cream ice cream

**Ingredients for the topping:**

- Hot fudge, for drizzling
- Oreos, crushed and for topping

HHHHHHHHHHHHHHHHHHHHHHHHHHHHHHHHHHH

**Instructions:**

1. Preheat the oven to 325 degrees. Grease a springform pan with cooking spray.

2. In a bowl, add in the ingredients for the brownie layer. Stir well to mix. Prepare half of the brownie batter according to the directions on the package. Remove the brownies and set aside to cool for 1 hour.

3. Prepare the cookie dough layer. In a bowl, add in the melted butter, white sugar and light brown sugar. Beat with an electric mixer until smooth in consistency. Add in the whole milk, pure vanilla, white flour and salt. Continue to beat until fluffy in consistency. Add in the miniature chocolate chips. Fold gently to mix.

4. Press the cookie dough layer into the bottom of the springform pan.

5. Add a layer of Oreo cookies over the cookie dough layer. Drizzle with the hot fudge.

6. Add a layer of the cookies and cream ice cream.

7. Cover and place into the freezer to chill for 1 hour.

8. Press the baked brownies over the ice cream layer. Spread the remaining half gallon of ice cream over this layer. Drizzle the hot fudge over the top.

9. Cover and place into the freezer to chill for 6 hours.

10. Remove and serve.

# Recipe 8: Oreo Chocolate Candy Bar Brownies

Make this delicious treat for those picky eaters in your household. It is so easy to make, you can get the entire family in on the fun.

**Yield:** 24 servings

**Preparation Time:** 30 minutes

**Ingredient List:**

- 1, 18 to 20 ounce pack of brownie mix
- 1, 3.4 ounce Oreo candy bay, chopped

HHHHHHHHHHHHHHHHHHHHHHHHHHHHHHHHHHHH

**Instructions:**

1. Prepare the pack of brownie mix according to the directions on the package. Once baked, set the brownies aside to cool for 5 minutes.

2. Top off with the chopped Oreo candy bar, pressing gently into the surface.

3. Slice into wedges and serve.

# Recipe 9: Hot Fudge Cheesecake Bars

This is a dish that will become every chocolate lover's dream. This is the perfect dish to make whenever you need to make a special treat for your entire family to enjoy.

**Yield:** 12 servings

**Preparation Time:** 4 hours

**Ingredients for the crust:**

- 24 Oreos, crushed
- 6 Tablespoons of butter, melted
- Dash of salt

**Ingredients for the cheesecake:**

- 2, 8 ounce bars of cream cheese, soft
- ½ cup of white sugar
- ¼ cup of light brown sugar
- ¼ cup of powdered cocoa
- 2 eggs
- 1 teaspoon of pure vanilla
- Dash of salt
- 1 cup of hot fudge sauce, extra for garnish
- ½ cup of Oreos, chopped and for garnish

HHHHHHHHHHHHHHHHHHHHHHHHHHHHHHHHHHHH

**Instructions:**

1. Preheat the oven to 325 degrees. Grease a baking dish with cooking spray.

2. Prepare the crust. In a bowl, add in the crushed Oreos, melted butter and salt. Stir well until evenly mixed. Press into the baking dish tightly.

3. Prepare the cheesecake filling. In a bowl, add in the bars of cream cheese, white sugar, light brown sugar and powdered cocoa. Beat with an electric mixer until fluffy in consistency. Add in the eggs, pure vanilla and salt. Beat again until smooth in consistency. Add in the fudge sauce and fold gently to mix.

4. Pour the filling over the crust.

5. Place into the oven to bake for 40 minutes. Remove and cool. Cover and place into the fridge to chill for 3 hours.

6. Drizzle extra hot fudge sauce over the top. Garnish with the chopped Oreos.

7. Slice into bars and serve immediately.

# Recipe 10: Oreo Truffles

This is another delicious truffle dish that is perfect to make right in time for the holiday season. Made with Oreos and white chocolate, this is a dish that came straight from heaven.

**Yield:** 12 servings

**Preparation Time:** 1 hour and 5 minutes

**Ingredient List:**

- 1 pack of Oreos
- 1, 8 ounce pack of soft cream cheese
- 12 ounces of white chocolate chips, melted

## Instructions:

1. In a Ziploc bag, add in the Oreos. Seal the bag and crush the cookies with a rolling pin until the fine in consistency.

2. Place a sheet of parchment paper onto a baking sheet.

3. In a bowl, add in the soft cream cheese and Oreo crumbs, making sure to reserve ¼ cup of the crumbs. Stir well to mix.

4. Shape the mix into 30 balls that are 1 inch in size. Place onto the baking sheet. Transfer the baking sheet into the freezer to chill for 30 minutes.

5. Dip the balls in the melted white chocolate chips until coated on all sides. Place back onto the baking sheet. Sprinkle the remaining crumbled Oreos over the top immediately.

6. Place back into the freezer to chill for 15 minutes or until hard.

7. Serve.

# Recipe 11: Mint Oreo Bark

This is a dish that you wouldn't think can become addicting, but once you try it for yourself, you won't be able to help but become hooked.

**Yield:** 8 to 10 servings

**Preparation Time:** 3 hours and 10 minutes

**Ingredient List:**

- 25 ounces of white chocolate chips
- 1 teaspoon of coconut oil
- Green food coloring, as needed
- 20 Oreos, crushed and evenly divided
- 1 teaspoon of peppermint extract
- ½ cup of semisweet chocolate chips, melted

HHHHHHHHHHHHHHHHHHHHHHHHHHHHHHHHHHHH

**Instructions:**

1. Place a sheet of parchment paper onto a baking sheet.

2. In a bowl, add in the white chocolate chips, coconut oil and 2 to 3 drops of green food coloring. Place into the microwave to cook for 30 seconds to 1 minute or until fully melted. Stir well to evenly blend.

3. Add in ¾ of the crushed Oreos and peppermint extract. Fold gently to mix.

4. Pour into the baking dish.

5. Top off with a layer of crushed Oreos and a drizzle of the melted chocolate.

6. Cover and place into the fridge to chill for 3 hours or until hard.

7. Break into pieces and serve.

# Recipe 12: Fried Oreos

If you have never tried fried cookies before, then this is one dish I know you are going to love. Often served at state fairs, this is an easy sweet treat you can make from the comfort of your own home.

**Yield:** 16 servings

**Preparation Time:** 40 minutes

**Ingredients for the oreos:**

- 1, 16 ounce bottle of vegetable oil
- 1 cup of bisquick
- 1 cup of funfetti cake mix
- 1 cup of whole milk
- 1 teaspoon of pure vanilla
- 2 eggs
- 1 pack of Oreos

**Ingredients for the glaze:**

- 1 cup of powdered sugar
- ¼ cup of buttermilk
- 1/3 cup of rainbow sprinkles

HHHHHHHHHHHHHHHHHHHHHHHHHHHHHHHHHH

**Instructions:**

1. Prepare the Oreos. In a skillet set over medium to high heat, add in the vegetable oil.

2. In a bowl, add in the Bisquick, funfetti cake mix, whole milk, pure vanilla and eggs. Beat with an electric mixer until smooth in consistency.

3. Using tongs, dip the Oreo cookies into the cake mix. Drop immediately into the hot oil. Fry for 2 minutes or until golden on both sides. Place onto a plate lined with paper towels to drain. Repeat with the remaining Oreos.

4. Prepare the glaze. In a bowl, add in the powdered sugar and buttermilk. Whisk well until smooth in consistency. Drizzle over the Oreos.

5. Sprinkle the rainbow sprinkles over the top. Serve.

# Recipe 13: Oreo Cheesecake Waffles

These waffles are the perfect way to start off your morning. Best of all, these waffles are so delicious, they will please even the pickiest of eaters in your home.

**Yield:** 2 servings

**Preparation Time:** 30 minutes

**Ingredients for the waffles:**

- 2 cups of white flour
- ½ cup of white sugar
- 1 tablespoon of baker's style baking powder
- 2 Tablespoons of powdered cocoa
- 1 teaspoon of salt
- 2 eggs
- 1 ½ cups of whole milk
- 8 Tablespoons of butter, melted
- 20 Oreo cookies, crushed

**Ingredients for the cheesecake:**

- 8 ounces of soft cream cheese
- 1 cup of heavy whipping cream
- ½ cup of powdered sugar
- 8 Oreo cookies, chopped
- Whipped cream, for topping

HHHHHHHHHHHHHHHHHHHHHHHHHHHHHHHHHHH

**Instructions:**

1. Preheat a waffle iron to medium or high heat.

2. In a bowl, add in the white flour, white sugar, baker's style baking powder, powdered cocoa and dash of salt. Stir well to mix.

3. Add in the eggs, whole milk and melted butter. Stir well until just mixed. Add in the crushed Oreos and fold gently to mix.

4. Pour 1/3 cup of the batter onto the waffle iron. Close the lid and cook for 5 minutes or until the waffles are golden. Transfer onto a plate and repeat.

5. In a bowl, add in the soft cream cheese. Beat with an electric mixer until smooth in consistency. Add in the heavy whipping cream and powdered sugar. Continue to beat until peaks begin to form on the surface.

6. Spread the cheesecake onto one waffle. Top off with a second waffle. Repeat and stack the waffles on top of each other.

7. Top the waffles off with the chopped Oreos and whipped cream. Serve immediately.

# Recipe 14: Oreo Ice Cream Tart

This is another delicious treat you can serve to celebrate your friends and family's birthdays. One bite and everyone will become hooked.

**Yield:** 6 servings

**Preparation Time:** 40 minutes

**Ingredient List:**

- 30 Oreo cookies, frosting removed
- 1 stick of butter, melted
- 12 scoops of cookies and cream ice cream
- 2 Cookies and Crème bars, melted
- Chocolate sauce, for drizzling

**Instructions:**

1. In a food processor, add in the Oreo cookies. Pulse on the highest setting until crumbly in consistency. Ad in the melted butter and pulse again until mixed.

2. Transfer the cookie mix into a springform pan. Cover and place into the freezer to freeze for 30 minutes.

3. Pour the ice cream over the crust.

4. Drizzle the melted chocolate bar over the ice cream.

5. Drizzle the chocolate sauce over the top.

6. Slice into pieces and serve immediately.

# Recipe 15: Hot Cocoa Cheesecake

This is a delicious cheesecake dish that is absolutely irresistible. Just like regular hot cocoa, this is a dish that you can make during those cold winter night when you need to be warmed up.

**Yield:** 8 to 10 servings

**Preparation Time:** 8 hours

## Ingredients for the crust:

- 24 Oreos, whole
- 6 Tablespoons of butter, melted
- Dash of salt

## Ingredients for the filling:

- 3, 8 ounce blocks of cream cheese, soft
- 2 packs of hot cocoa mix
- ¾ cup of white sugar
- 3 eggs
- ¼ cup of sour cream
- 1 teaspoon of pure vanilla
- ½ teaspoons of salt

## Ingredients for the topping:

- 15 marshmallows
- 2 Tablespoons of powdered cocoa, for garnish

HHHHHHHHHHHHHHHHHHHHHHHHHHHHHHHHHHHH

**Instructions:**

1. Preheat the oven to 325 degrees. Grease a springform pan with cooking spray.

2. Prepare the crust. In a bowl, add in the Oreos, melted butter and dash of salt. Stir well until moist. Press into the springform pan.

3. Prepare the filling. In a bowl, add in the blocks of cream cheese, packs of hot cocoa mix and white sugar. Beat with an electric mixer until smooth in consistency. Add in the eggs, sour cream, pure vanilla and dash of salt. Continue to beat until fluffy in consistency.

4. Pour the filling over the crust.

5. Wrap the outside of the pan with two sheets of aluminum foil. Place into a baking dish. Pour water into the baking dish, making sure it goes up to halfway up the springform pan.

6. Place into the oven to bake for 1 hour and 25 minutes. Turn off the oven and open the door. Allow the cheesecake to sit in the oven for 1 hour.

7. Remove and place into the fridge to chill for 5 hours.

8. Prepare the topping. Place a sheet of parchment paper onto a baking sheet. Place the marshmallows over the top. Place into the oven to broil for 1 minute or until golden.

9. Place the marshmallows on top of the cheesecake. Sprinkle the powdered cocoa over the top.

10. Slice into wedges and serve.

# Recipe 16: Oreo Pumpkin Bars

These are the perfect bars to make right in time for the fall season. Make these bars with freshly picked pumpkins for the tastiest results.

**Yield:** 12 servings

**Preparation Time:** 4 hours and 15 minutes

**Ingredient List:**

- 1 box of brownie mix + ingredients listed on the box
- 12 ounces of soft cream cheese
- 2/3 cup of pumpkin
- 2/3 cup of white sugar
- 2 eggs
- 1 teaspoon of pure vanilla
- ½ teaspoons of pumpkin pie spice
- Dash of salt
- 15 Oreo cookies, extra for topping
- Caramel sauce, for drizzling

HHHHHHHHHHHHHHHHHHHHHHHHHHHHHHHHHH

**Instructions:**

1. Preheat the oven to 325 degrees. Place a sheet of parchment paper into a baking dish.

2. Pour the prepared brownie batter into the baking dish. Top off with a layer of the Oreo cookies.

3. Prepare the filling. In a bowl, add in the soft cream cheese, pumpkin pie spice, white sugar, eggs, pure vanilla, pumpkin and salt. Beat with an electric mixer until smooth in consistency. Pour over the cookie mix in the baking dish.

4. Top off with the crushed Oreos.

5. Place into the oven to bake for 50 minutes.

6. Remove. Cover and place into the fridge to chill for 3 hours.

7. Drizzle the caramel over the top. Slice into bars and serve.

# Recipe 17: Skillet Oreo Brownie

This is the ultimate decadent treat that is perfect to serve during your next girl's night out. One bite and your girlfriends will be begging you for the recipe.

**Yield:** 8 servings

**Preparation Time:** 50 minutes

**Ingredient List:**

- 1 pack of Pillsbury chocolate chip cookie dough
- 18 Oreos, crushed and extra for topping
- 1 box of brownie mix + ingredients listed on the box
- Vanilla ice cream, for serving

**Instructions:**

1. Preheat the oven to 350 degrees. Grease a cast iron skillet with baking spray.

2. Press the roll of cookie dough into the bottom of the skillet. Add a layer of Crushed Oreos over the top.

3. Prepare the brownie batter according to the directions on the package. Pour 2/3 of the batter over the Oreos in the skillet. Repeat these layers twice, topping off with extra crushed Oreos.

4. Place into the oven to bake for 35 minutes or until the cake is slightly mushy.

5. Remove and set aside to cool for 20 minutes.

6. Serve with a topping of vanilla ice cream.

# Recipe 18: Chocolate Oreo Cookie Cake

Make this delicious Oreo cookie cake whenever you need to celebrate someone's birthday. One bite and everybody will want you to make this cake every year.

**Yield:** 16 servings

**Preparation Time:** 1 hour and 20 minutes

**Ingredient List:**

- 1 pack of devil food cake mic
- 1, 4 ounce pack of semi-sweet chocolate
- ¼ cup of butter
- 1, 8 ounce pack of soft cream cheese
- ½ cup of white sugar
- 2 cups of cool whip
- 12 Oreo cookies, crushed

HHHHHHHHHHHHHHHHHHHHHHHHHHHHHHHHHH

**Instructions:**

1. Heat the oven to 350 degrees.

2. Prepare the devil food cake according to the directions on the package using two cake pans. Once cakes are baked, set aside to cool completely.

3. In a bowl, add in the semi-sweet chocolate and butter. Microwave for 45 minutes or until melted. Stir well to mix.

4. In a separate bowl, add in the cream cheese and white sugar. Beat with an electric mixer until smooth in consistency. Add in the cool whip and crushed Oreos. Continue to beat until smooth.

5. Place one cake onto a plate. Spread the cream cheese mix over the cake. Top off with the remaining cake. Spread the chocolate glaze over the top.

6. Set aside to rest for 10 minutes. Serve immediately.

# Recipe 19: Peppermint and Oreo Truffles

This is an Oreo dish that is so simple to make, you won't believe it until you try it. It is the perfect treat to make just in time for the Christmas season.

**Yield:** 20 servings

**Preparation Time:** 45 minutes

**Ingredient List:**

- 1, 15.5 ounce pack of Oreos, crushed
- 1, 8 ounce pack of cream cheese, soft
- 12 candy canes, crushed and evenly divided
- 2 cups of chocolate chips, melted
- 2 teaspoons of coconut oil

HHHHHHHHHHHHHHHHHHHHHHHHHHHHHHHHHHHHH

**Instructions:**

1. Place a sheet of parchment paper onto a baking sheet.

2. In a bowl, add in the crushed Oreos, soft cream cheese and half of the crushed candy canes. Stir well until evenly blended.

3. Shape the Oreo mix into small balls. Place onto a baking sheet.

4. Transfer into the freezer to chill for 10 minutes.

5. In a bowl, add in the coconut oil and melted chocolate chips. Stir well until evenly mixed. Dip the balls into the chocolate and place back onto the baking sheet.

6. Sprinkle the remaining crushed candy canes over the balls.

7. Place back into the freezer to freeze for 10 minutes before serving.

# Recipe 20: Oreo Coal

While coal is primarily for those who misbehave, nobody would mind getting this type of coal in their stocking come Christmas Day.

**Yield:** 38 to 40 servings

**Preparation Time:** 1 hour and 15 minutes

**Ingredient List:**

- 40 Oreos
- 1, 8 ounce block of cream cheese, soft
- 1, 16 ounce bar of semisweet chocolate, melted
- 1/3 cup of Oreo cookies, crushed

HHHHHHHHHHHHHHHHHHHHHHHHHHHHHHHHHHH

**Instructions:**

1. In a food processor, add in the Oreos. Pulse on the highest setting until crumbled. Transfer into a bowl. In the bowl, add in the soft cream cheese. Stir well until mixed.

2. Shape the mix into cookies that are 1 inch in size. Transfer onto a baking sheet lined with a sheet of parchment paper. Place into the fridge to chill for 1 hour.

3. In a bowl, add in the chocolate. Melt in the microwave for 30 seconds to 1 minute.

4. Dip the balls of dough into the chocolate. Place back onto the baking sheet.

5. Immediately sprinkle the crushed Oreos over the top.

6. Place back into the fridge to chill for an additional 20 minutes. Remove and serve.

# Recipe 21: Brownie Oreo Pie

How can you go wrong with a pie crush that is made out of cookie dough? This is one dish that is perfect for those who need to indulge themselves this weekend.

**Yield:** 8 servings

**Preparation Time:** 4 hours and 25 minutes

**Ingredients for the crust:**

- 1 tube of premade chocolate chip cookie dough

**Ingredients for the pudding:**

- 2/3 pack of instant chocolate pudding mix
- 1 ½ cup of whole milk
- 1 pack of Oreo cookies

**Ingredients for the whipped cream:**

- 1, 8 ounce container of cool whip
- 1/3 pack of instant chocolate pudding mix
- ½ cup of brownie pieces, crumbled
- Chocolate sauce, for drizzling

HHHHHHHHHHHHHHHHHHHHHHHHHHHHHHHHHHHH

**Instructions:**

1. Preheat the oven to 350 degrees. Grease a pie plate with cooking spray.

2. Prepare the crust. Press the cookie dough into the pie plate. Place into the oven to bake for 15 to 20 minutes or until baked through. Remove and set into the fridge to chill.

3. Prepare the pudding. In a bowl, add in the chocolate pudding mix and whole milk. Whisk well until mixed. Place into the fridge to set for 5 minutes before pouring into the cookie crust.

4. Place a layer of Oreo cookies over the pudding mix.

5. In a separate bowl, add in the cool whip and the remaining 1/3 pack of pudding mix. Add in the crumbled brownie pieces. Fold gently to incorporate. Pour into the pie plate.

6. Garnish the pie plate with extra brownie pieces.

7. Cover and place into the fridge to chill for 4 hours.

8. Drizzle the chocolate sauce over the top and serve.

# Recipe 22: Oreo and Peanut Butter Cheesecake

This is a delicious Oreo and Peanut Butter Cheesecake dish you can make whenever you need to spoil yourself with something sweet. Made with the ultimate combination of peanut butter and Oreos, this is a treat you will want to make as often as possible.

**Yield:** 16 servings

**Preparation Time:** 5 hours and 20 minutes

**Ingredient List:**

- 1, 15.5 ounce pack of Oreo cookies, evenly divided
- 3 Tablespoons of butter, melted
- 3, 8 ounce packs of soft cream cheese
- ¾ cup of white sugar
- 1, 16 ounce container of sour cream
- 1 cup of creamy peanut butter
- 3 eggs

HHHHHHHHHHHHHHHHHHHHHHHHHHHHHHHHHHH

**Instructions:**

1. Heat the oven to 350 degrees.

2. Crush 16 of the Oreos. Chop the remaining Oreos.

3. In a bowl, add in the Oreo crumbs and melted butter. Stir well to mix. Press into the bottom of a cheesecake pan.

4. In a bowl, add in the packs of cream cheese and white sugar. Beat with an electric mixer until smooth in consistency. Add in the sour cream and peanut butter. Add in the eggs and continue to beat until fluffy in consistency. Add in the chopped Oreos. Fold gently to mix.

5. Pour the batter over the crust.

6. Place into the oven to bake for 1 hour or until the center is set.

7. Remove and place into the fridge to chill for 4 hours before serving.

# Recipe 23: Triple Layer Mud Pie

This is a pie dish that every chocoholic will be envious of. It is made with three layers of chocolate and pecans to make the ultimate dessert dish everyone will love.

**Yield:** 10 servings

**Preparation Time:** 3 hours and 15 minutes

**Ingredient List:**

- 3 ounces of semi-sweet chocolate, melted
- ¼ cup of canned condensed milk
- 1, 6 ounce Oreo pie crust
- ½ cup of pecans, chopped and toasted
- 2, 3.9 ounce packs of instant chocolate pudding mix
- 2 cups of 2% milk
- 1, 8 ounce container of cool whip, evenly divided

HHHHHHHHHHHHHHHHHHHHHHHHHHHHHHHHHHH

**Instructions:**

1. In a bowl, add in the melted chocolate and can of condensed milk. Stir well to mix. Pour into the Oreo pie crust.

2. Sprinkle the chopped toasted pecans over the top.

3. In a separate bowl, add in the packs of instant chocolate pudding mix and 2% milk. Beat well to mix. Pour over the pecans in the pie crust.

4. In the remaining pudding, add half of the cool whip. Fold well to incorporate. Spread over the pudding layer.

5. Pour the remaining cool whip over the top.

6. Cover and place into the fridge to chill for 3 hours.

# Recipe 24: Oreo Cheesecake Bites

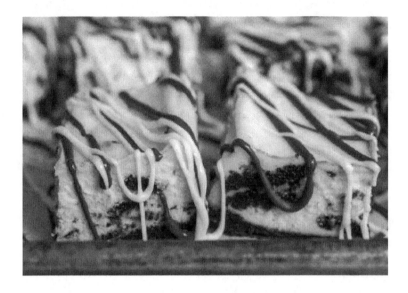

This is the perfect dessert dish for you to make whenever you want to show off your baking skills. It is so delicious; your friends and family will be begging you for the recipe.

**Yield:** 36 servings

**Preparation Time:** 5 hours and 5 minutes

**Ingredient List:**

- 36 Oreos, evenly divided
- ½ cup of butter, evenly divided
- 4, 8 ounce packs of cream cheese, soft
- 1 cup of white sugar
- 1 cup of sour cream
- 1 teaspoon of pure vanilla
- 4 eggs
- 1, 4 ounce pack of semi-sweet chocolate

HHHHHHHHHHHHHHHHHHHHHHHHHHHHHHHHHHH

**Instructions:**

1. Preheat the oven to 325 degrees.

2. Place a sheet of aluminum foil into a baking dish.

3. In a bowl, add in 24 of the Oreos. Crush finely. Add in ¼ cup of the butter. Stir well to mix. Press into the baking dish.

4. In a bowl, add in the packs of cream cheese and white sugar. Beat with an electric mixer until smooth in consistency. Add in the sour cream, pure vanilla and eggs. Continue to beat until fluffy in consistency.

5. Chop the remaining Oreo cookies. Add into the batter and fold gently to incorporate.

6. Pour into the baking dish.

7. Place into the oven to bake for 45 minutes or until set. Remove and set aside to cool.

8. In a bowl, add in the chocolate and remaining butter. Microwave until the chocolate is melted. Stir well to mix. Spread over the top of the cheesecake.

9. Cover and place into the fridge to chill for 4 hours.

10. Slice into bars and serve.

# Recipe 25: Gold Oreo Truffles

These small truffles make for the perfect celebratory dessert. Topped off with golden sprinkles, these truffles make for the perfect treat to serve during your next bridal or baby shower.

**Yield:** 40 servings

**Preparation Time:** 2 hours

**Ingredient List:**

- 1, 14 ounce pack of Golden Oreos
- 8 ounces of soft cream cheese
- 12 ounces of white chocolate, chopped
- Gold sprinkles, for topping

HHHHHHHHHHHHHHHHHHHHHHHHHHHHHHHHHHHHHH

**Instructions:**

1. In a food processor, add in the Oreos. Pulse until crumbly in consistency. Transfer into a bowl.

2. In the bowl, add in the soft cream cheese. Beat with an electric mixer until smooth in consistency.

3. Roll the cookie mix into 40 balls that are 1 inch in size. Place onto a baking sheet lined with a sheet of parchment paper. Place into the fridge to chill for 30 minutes.

4. Add the chopped white chocolate into a bowl. Microwave for 30 seconds to 1 minute or until fully melted.

5. Dip the truffle balls into the melted chocolate. Immediately sprinkle the gold sprinkles over the top.

6. Transfer back onto the baking sheet. Set into the fridge to chill for 5 to 10 minutes before serving.

# About the Author

Angel Burns learned to cook when she worked in the local seafood restaurant near her home in Hyannis Port in Massachusetts as a teenager. The head chef took Angel under his wing and taught the young woman the tricks of the trade for cooking seafood. The skills she had learned at a young age helped her get accepted into Boston University's Culinary Program where she also minored in business administration.

Summers off from school meant working at the same restaurant but when Angel's mentor and friend retired as head chef, she took over after graduation and created classic and new dishes that delighted the diners. The restaurant flourished under Angel's culinary creativity and one customer developed more than an appreciation for Angel's food. Several months after taking over the position, the young woman met her future husband at work and they have been inseparable ever since. They still live in Hyannis Port with their two children and a cocker spaniel named Buddy.

Angel Burns turned her passion for cooking and her business acumen into a thriving e-book business. She has authored several successful books on cooking different types of dishes using simple ingredients for novices and experienced chefs alike. She is still head chef in Hyannis Port and says she will probably never leave!

♥ ♣ ♥ ♥ ♥ ♥ ♣ ♥ ♣ ♥ ♣ ♥ ♥ ♥ ♥ ♣ ♥ ♣ ♥ ♥ ♥ ♥ ♥ ♣ ♥

# Author's Afterthoughts

With so many books out there to choose from, I want to thank you for choosing this one and taking precious time out of your life to buy and read my work. Readers like you are the reason I take such passion in creating these books.

It is with gratitude and humility that I express how honored I am to become a part of your life and I hope that you take the same pleasure in reading this book as I did in writing it.

Can I ask one small favour? I ask that you write an honest and open review on Amazon of what you thought of the book. This will help other readers make an informed choice on whether to buy this book.

*My sincerest thanks,*

*Angel Burns*

If you want to be the first to know about news, new books, events and giveaways, subscribe to my newsletter by clicking the link below

*https://angel-burns.gr8.com*

**or Scan QR-code**

Made in the USA
San Bernardino,
CA